My Ancestors' Village

By Roberta Labastida

Dedicated to the Kumeyaay children of San Diego and Baja California

And to Marcus, Dominic and Sophia

My Ancestors' Village

Copyright © 2004 by the author

Sunbelt Publications, Inc.
All rights reserved. First edition 2004
Edited by Diana Lindsay
Book and cover design by Leah Cooper
Project management by Jennifer Redmond
Printed in the United States of America

**Publication of this book made possible through the
generous support of the Barona Band of Mission Indians.**

No part of this book may be reproduced in any form without permission of the publisher. Please direct comments and inquiries to:

Sunbelt Publications, Inc.
P.O. Box 191126
San Diego, CA 92159-1126
(619) 258-4911, fax: (619) 258-4916
mail@sunbeltpub.com
www.sunbeltbooks.com

07 06 05 04 03   5 4 3 2 1

Library of Congress Cataloging-in-Publication Data

Labastida, Roberta.
    My ancestors' village / by Roberta Labastida.-- 1st ed.
        p. cm.
    Summary: Describes the life of a Kumeyaay, or Kamia, Indian girl and her family living in San Diego area long ago. Includes a glossary of Kumeyaay words and a clarification of the different Indian groups from this area.
    ISBN 0-932653-61-8
        1. Kamia Indians--Juvenile literature. 2. Indians of North America--California--Juvenile literature. [1. Kamia Indians. 2. Indians of North America--California.] I. Title.

E99.K18 L33 2003
305.897'572--dc22
2003015812

What is the Name of this Tribe?
A Lesson in San Diego County's Indian History

The Indians of San Diego County are often divided into these language groups: Cahuilla, Cupeño, Kumeyaay, and Luiseño. The origin of the names of local tribes is complex due to history and political organization of the tribes. Some of the names tribes have today reflect the reservation they live on, and many names are from someone else's language. According to anthropologists, some names reflect a language group or a dialect in the people's language. The Spanish, Mexicans, or Americans named some groups, and several tribes have names that are in the language of the neighboring tribe. The Yuman family group, commonly referred to as Kumeyaay, is perhaps the most challenging with names that include: Diegueño, Mission, Northern Diegueño, Southern Diegueño, 'Iipay (Ipai), Tiipay (Tipai), Metiipay, Kamia, Kumiai, and Kumeyaay.

The southern California Yuman language groups called themselves "the people." There are three languages: 'Iipay, Tiipay, and Kumeyaay. At the beginning of the mission era, the Spanish named the Indians of San Diego the Diegueño for the San Diego Mission. Only the people living near the coast were missionized, but the name stayed for most of the Indians in the San Diego area. Eventually the federal government included the name "mission" in the names of many of the

California bands. Barona, for example, is called the "Barona Band of Mission Indians," even though the Barona people were never in the mission system.

Another name for the Barona people that is more accurate is 'Iipay. This is the name of the language spoken by the people in north county, also called the Northern Diegueño. In south county and Baja California, the people spoke two languages: Tiipay and Kumeyaay. 'Iipay and Tiipay are translated as "the people." Kumeyaay may mean "the ones who are together" or "the steep ones from the cliffs." The languages used by these groups can vary as a result of intermarriage and other sociopolitical factors. The word list at the back of the book reflects several of these languages.

In the 1970s, the name Kumeyaay was adopted by some of the Indians in San Diego County. They wanted to emphasize to non-Indians that they are an organized group of people — a political force. However, there are some people such as the 'Iipay who feel that this designation does not fit them. The people living in the south may more often accept the term Kumeyaay. People who have relatives from both language groups may also accept it. Therefore, it depends on whom you talk to whether this is an appropriate term for that person's heritage.

— Cheryl Hinton, Director/Curator,
The Barona Cultural Center and Museum
of the Barona Band of Mission Indians

My Ancestors' Village

Haáwka! My name is *Kilyaahwii* (Dove). You might know me as a Kumeyaay Indian because I lived many years ago in a mountain valley near here in what is San Diego County today. In the past we were known by our own name, 'lipay, and that is the name my people still call themselves. My home could have been where your house is right now! Sometimes when you're playing near streams, around boulders, or under a very old oak tree, you may find shards (fragments) of pottery. Those could have been pieces of the very pots that my family used to cook in or store our food in.

I want you to know my family and the way we lived long ago. This is Dragonfly, my father. New Moon is my mother. My brother is called *Paasuly*, which means Little Brother in your language. Born by Rock is my grandmother and Raven Wing is my grandfather. My cousin is not here now, but we will see him soon.

This is our village. We live near a stream that runs through the valley. It is so beautiful here. Many oak trees give us shade, and also acorns to eat. Willow trees grow here, and there are many rabbits, squirrel, and deer. We have all that we need. My grandfather says, as long as we have water, we will want for nothing. The water is good for plants and animals and my people.

I think we live in the best valley. Yes, it is wonderful here.

My little cousin '*Ephar* (Brush Rabbit) is visiting us from his village near the ocean. My aunt and uncle live there and have come to trade shells and fish with us and the other villages farther east. It's so exciting having traders and relatives come to visit. Some of the villages are in the desert, others in the mountains, others are many miles away to the north and the south. We have relatives in most of the villages and share the same language and ceremonies. Our *kwaypaay* (leader/captain) invites other tribes to visit for special occasions. The whole village prepares food and gets things ready for the visitors. It is good to see our family and friends and to hear the news from other areas.

Do you see my 'ewaa (house)? It is made from willow branches full of leaves, woven and tied to a pole frame. It takes two or more people working together to build the house. My 'ewaa keeps us safe from the rain and the winds. It is a warm place for sleeping. We cook outside on an open fire. Sometimes, if it is very cold, we build a small fire in the hut, and we sleep on rabbit fur blankets. It is nice to sleep with my mother, father, and brother. I feel warm and safe.

The willow tree not only gives us her branches to make our houses and baskets but also her bark and leaves for cradle boards, medicine, and clothing. Do you see my skirt? It is made from willow bark. Did you know you could make a skirt from bark? It is very soft, and we use it to pad the baby's cradle boards.

I love the smell of the willow tree, and I like to lie in the cool shade. This is where my friends and I come to play. Just like you, we like to play games and run races. My mother and grandmother made me little jars and baskets and a clay doll. I made some little dishes and baskets too. I want to learn to be like my mother.

One day I cut willow branches and made a cradle board for my doll just like my mother did for Paasuly. Then I could carry my doll with me when I played. I tore willow bark and made a nice soft padding so she would be comfortable and tied her in with yucca strips to keep her safe.

Father made Paasuly a little bow with arrows. The little boys of the tribe try to be hunters just like their fathers. They practice shooting the little arrows at targets and live animals.

The boys and girls love to run races. This is very good practice for them because we need runners to carry news from one tribe to another. The runners are strong and take messages from the desert to the ocean and far to the north and south.

There is another running game where the participants kick a wooden or rock ball back and forth for miles and then run back again.

The boys also play a game by throwing long sticks through hoops to get points.

The women play a dice game using four decorated sticks that they toss. The score is counted by which side lands up or down.

When I came home from playing, I saw that my mother was worried. Paasuly had become very hot and wouldn't eat. We knew he was sick. I was afraid. My mother boiled some willow bark in water and gave a little of the willow drink to him. He rested and soon became better. My mother thanked the tree for giving us the medicine. It is our way, to always thank the trees for giving us so many things. We tell the tree we will only use as many branches, leaves or as much bark as we will need. Today in your world, aspirin is made from willow.

Many plants are used for medicine and many plants are used for food. Special people in my village know the ways of plants. The *kuseyaay* (doctor/shaman) takes care of us with the plant medicine and uses his special powers during special ceremonies or prayers to remove sickness.

My grandmother also knows the ways of medicine and is teaching me. She is an elder. Elders are people who have lived long and have learned and are very wise. We respect the elders. They are our teachers.

My mother and grandmother teach me how to look for and gather food for our family. Everyone in the village works hard to gather and prepare the food. We collect the foods as the seasons provide them.

Beginning in early to late summer the piñon nuts from pine trees are ripe. In the fall the acorns drop from the oak trees. There are many live oaks here, but many of us travel high into the mountains to gather the black oak acorns that are so big and good. The piñon nuts are an important food source for us, and they can be eaten right away. We can eat them raw, right out of the shell, toasted, or added to our stew.

When we gather acorns and piñon nuts, we carry as many as we can and bring them back to our village. We store the acorns in a huge granary basket made from leafy willow branches that protect the acorns from insects. It sits in the crook of a tree or on a support to keep it off the ground so the acorns won't get wet.

Do you see how the trees keep providing for us?

In the spring and summer we gather seeds, bulbs, roots, flowers, herbs, and cactus to add to our meals. We eat these like you eat vegetables. These can be eaten raw, brewed into teas, or steamed and eaten with our *shawii* (acorn mush) or meat. Our mouths turn purple eating the ripe cactus fruit and the berries.

The men travel to the desert to gather *'emally* (agave/mescal) plants, another of our favorite foods. The agave needs to be harvested while the new stem is still sweet. Our kuseyaay knows just when they must go to dig it up. He watches the stars and weather, and at just the right time he sends the men to gather the agave. They dig the big, thick, juicy agave stems and put them into rock lined pits dug into the ground. After the stem is covered with hot coals and cooked for a few days, it is taken out of the pit and pounded into thin layers, dried in the hot desert sun, and rolled to be carried back home. While in the desert, some of the men will hunt the bighorn sheep that roam the high mountain ranges.

There is so much to be done that we all need to help each other.

⊗

Keyiw! (come!) Grandfather is teaching my cousin 'Ephar how to hunt with a throwing stick. He has made a smaller stick for 'Ephar to throw at rocks and bushes. This is a good game for the children to play, and they learn the skills to be a good hunter.

Many in the village hunt for small animals like rabbits, squirrel, rats, lizards, and birds using throwing sticks or nets. The rabbit gives us nice meat to eat and fur for our blankets and cloaks. We only use that which we need and nothing is wasted.

Now Grandfather has gone back to finishing the arrow point he had started. He found a piece of shiny black obsidian in the desert, and now he is breaking small flakes off the sides with a piece of deer antler, shaping it carefully. He protects his legs from the sharp flakes with a scrap of deer hide. He needs to be very careful because the rock is very sharp, or it could crack and would be ruined. Grandfather also goes to the mountains and finds clear hard rocks to make his arrow points. His arrow points are admired by the men of our villages and are valuable for trading. There, he's done and he's pleased.

We make everything we need such as bows, arrows, throwing sticks, clothing, nets, pottery, and baskets. Our women are known for making beautiful, strong baskets. Baskets are made from different kinds of grasses and plants.

Let me show you how to make a strong juncus basket. First we gather the juncus plant along the stream edge, being careful not to poke ourselves with the sharp ends. We dry the juncus in the sun, then split it with our teeth into three long strips. We make a beginning base and begin to wrap the wet juncus strips around a small bunch of grass, poking a hole with an awl and pushing the juncus through it. Round and round the coil goes as we sew it to the next row. It takes a long time to make a juncus basket, but it is strong and will last a long time. Most of the baskets are used for storage and food preparation. Some of these baskets are round like plates. Others are like bowls and some are made to fit our heads.

Did you notice my hat? The basket hats are used for protection. When we use our carrying nets, these basket hats protect our hair and foreheads from the tumpline, the strap that supports the net to the head. The basket hat also looks pretty.

We cook our stews and shawii in these baskets. To make the shawii, we let the acorns dry in the sun until the shells are broken easily. We crack the shells and remove the acorn seeds. Then we winnow the brown skin off of the seeds by rubbing them in our hands and tossing them in this flat woven basket. When they are white and clean, we put them in one of the *'ehmuu* (mortar holes). We use an *esally* (pestle or long stone) to break the seeds into tiny pieces. We sift the pieces with a loose basket and gather the finely ground seeds. Acorns are very bitter because of tannic acid. It tastes awful. To make it tasty, we pour water over the ground acorn and soak the tannic acid out. After it is rinsed, it is ready to cook.

Next, we take a juncus basket and put the ground acorn and fresh water into it. We lift the stones from the fire with special sticks and add the hot stones to the mixture right in the basket, and then we stir them round and round. The water boils and cooks the shawii. Adding rabbit stew over the top makes it good. *Haa* (Yes), *'ehan* (it is good)!

Over here, near the stream is where we gather clay to make our pottery. Can you see the rich red mud? It is smooth and slippery. It smells like dirt after the rain. Haa, 'ehan!

Today my grandmother is making an *'aaskay* (olla or water jar). Some of our people believe that if someone watches you make an olla it will crack when it's fired. Keyiw, let's hide and see how she does it.

First, she grinds the clay on an *'ehpii* (metate or flat grinding stone) with a *hapiichaa* (mano or hand stone) to make it smooth, sifts it, adds sand, and then just enough water. Her hands knead the pile of soft red clay. She uses another jar as the base to start the new pot. She flattens a ball of clay in her hands and stretches it to fit the bottom of the olla she is using. Now she is rolling snakes of clay and adding these to the sides of the olla smoothing the edges with her fingers and thumbs. She carefully lifts the clay from the form and holds the new olla in her hands. Now gently she paddles the clay around the sides with a wooden paddle while her other hand is inside the jar with a clay anvil, or flat rock, that holds the sides steady. Carefully she adds more clay snakes while she is singing a song softly to the new jar that is being formed. There, the olla is done.

Oh, oh. This must be a special 'aaskay. Maybe it's to be a gift. My grandmother is preparing the red ochre paint to add designs to the olla. She uses a little yucca brush, made of fibers from the yucca plant, to paint lines down the sides. Some are straight and others are jagged. Now she puts her fingers in the paint and makes red dots on the jar. It is the prettiest 'aaskay I have seen. The olla must dry completely before it can be put in the ground fire. This will happen at night. That's our way. It is always fired at night.

We have a shallow pit ready. We line the bottom with dried yucca stalks and carefully lay the pottery pieces on this. Then we gently cover the pottery with more dried yucca stalks or oak branches. When the pottery is covered with the branches, we light the fire with leaves and small sticks until the soft dry wood begins to burn. The fire rises very fast and burns very hot for a few hours, then slowly it starts to go out. It cools overnight, and in the morning we take the pottery out to see if there are any cracks. Do you think my grandmother's beautiful olla has cracked because we have spied on her? 'Ehan! No cracks! The clay didn't see us peeking.

Our kwaypaay has called us all together for a gathering tonight. There will be singing, dancing and feasting around the campfire. Our kuseyaay will tell stories and sing songs that tell us how our world was made and why we are to respect and care for all that is given to us. Some of the men are singers and have learned the songs of our people. We have no written language like you do, so the stories and songs are memorized. The men will sing in time with the gourd rattles. Father will make 'Ephar a rattle like grandfather's so he will learn too when he is older.

Here comes the kuseyaay and the older girls from our village. They have finished a special ceremony to teach them the secrets of being good wives and mothers. Their chins have been tattooed to show that they are women now and not little girls. The kuseyaay had them pound their marks (cupules or small cup-like holes) on the rocks to please the ancestors and to have a good life. They are following the ways of our people. The kuseyaay reads the stars and seeks guidance from the ancestors. He paints symbols onto the rocks to honor the universe, nature, and our ancestors. We are one with all creation.

Grandmother says that soon I'll be a young woman, so she made me an olla. Haa! The beautiful painted 'aaskay. I am so happy it didn't crack.

I must go now to get ready and paint my face and arms with designs for the campfire tonight. This is our way of dressing up. I hope you enjoyed your visit to our village and hope you'll come again.

Remember, when you go outside to play, you are walking where my people walked. Take good care of all that has been given to us and waste nothing.

My people do not have a word for good-bye. We say, *'enyaach 'aamh* (I'm going). It would make me happy if you answered, *keyíma* (Go on then).

Author's Comments

The Kumeyaay lived/live throughout San Diego County, from northern Carlsbad to southern Ensenada, Baja California, and from the coast to near the Arizona border. They speak the Yuman language, which separates them from other surrounding Native American groups in San Diego County.

Their villages were near the beaches, valleys, mountains, and deserts. Because of the diversity of geography and weather, the Kumeyaay adapted certain skills, land management, and resources according to the area in which they lived.

The beliefs and cultural core were/are similar, with some varied, closely related languages that didn't interfere with communications between the groups of this Yuman speaking group. Grandparents, aunts, uncles, and cousins were scattered among the various villages because of food, marriage, territorial, and family needs. Yet, each band was run individually by their chosen leaders. They communicated news quickly from band to band by runners sent as messengers. Because of the distance between the villages, time, and political and historical interference, information may be different according to the sources used.

My Ancestors' Village uses the information I have learned through: the San Diego Museum of Man's Education Department; Virginia Landis; Ken Hedges; Jane Dumas; Mike Wilken; the late Florence Shipek; Melicent Lee's *Indian of the Oaks, Salt Water Boy, La-luck* and *Tuck-she of the Bush*; Krober's *California Indians*; and of course, many Kumeyaay friends and acquaintances from San Diego and Imperial counties and Baja California that I've met over the past ten years. I relied on old and new photographs, illustrations of Leslie W. Lee from *Indians of the Oaks*, and artifacts to guide my illustrations and make them as accurate as possible.

The original text for *My Ancestors' Village* was adapted to reflect the involvement of the Barona Cultural Center and Museum. Some of the Indian words used in this book were taken from the *Barona Tribal Dictionary*, some from the *Dictionary of Mesa Grande Diegueño*, and some were contributed by elders living in and near Barona. I would like to thank the Barona Band of Mission Indians for their assistance in the publication of this book, and Dr. Margaret Langdon for her fine work in linguistics among the San Diego County tribes. The accuracy and content was checked by Cheryl Hinton, Director of the Barona Cultural Center and Museum, and by Diana Lindsay of Sunbelt Publications.

Notes:

Page 5. The necklaces were made from shells traded with the Kumeyaay living near the ocean. There were many trading trails used to the north, south, east, and west. Grandfather is straightening an arrow shaft with a heated, grooved rock called an arrow straightener. Various woods were used to make the arrow shafts: willow, arrowweed, and manzanita.

Page 7. The grinding holes in the rocks are called mortars, and the pounding stone is called a pestle. The mortar and pestle can also be small portable rocks. Smooth areas on boulders called slicks are used for grinding seed using a round smooth stone called a mano. In a portable form, the slick is a stone called a metate. In the tree trunk is a granary basket that holds the acorns, which preserves them for many months. Pottery and basket containers were also used for storing smaller amounts of food. They kept extra rations of acorns hidden in case of food shortages or disasters.

Page 9. Kilyaahwii is carrying juncus, a rush plant that grows in wet, marshy areas and is used for basket material. The hut is willow, but could be made from tule, brush, or bark, depending on the area.

Page 11. There were many games played by children and adults. Peon is a gambling game still played today. There are two teams. One has the bones hidden in their hands and the other team tries to guess who is holding the bones. Rocks were used as jacks, and cord was used to play "Cat in the Cradle." Rock tossing games similar to lawn bowling were played as well as many running games.

Page 13. The bowl being used is an abalone shell with holes filled with sap or tar. Shells could be used for decoration or utilitarian purposes.

Page 15. The nets, tumplines, belts, sandals, and rope were made from fibrous plants like agave, yucca, or nettle. The berries being collected are manzanita berries, which were eaten fresh or dried, stored, and used as food or tea.

Page 17. Some resources say the stem of the agave was also used for food, and others say the heart of the plant was used. They all agree the time to dig the plant is before the flower blooms and takes all the sugar away from the stem/heart of the plant. The flowers were soaked to get rid of the bitter taste and were eaten raw or steamed. The buds of cactus were collected and eaten as well.

Page 19. Rabbit throwing sticks were a common hunting tool used among many Native American groups. Some of the rabbit sticks were decorated. The children imitated the adults around them by playing games using miniature hunting tools, which strengthened their ability to provide for their families. Children were encouraged to catch reptiles, rodents, and birds to be added to the family food supply. Arrow points were made from hard rock like volcanic rock, chert, quartz, and obsidian. Wooden points were also used for the arrow tip. These stones could also be made into scrapers, knives, and other cutting tools.

Page 21. Juncus and other reed type leaves and stems could be quickly woven into a loose disposable basket if one was needed for sifting or holding items. Elderberry and sumac were also used in weaving sturdy baskets.

Page 29. The Kumeyaay didn't use drums as other groups of Native Americans did. They accompanied their songs and ceremonies with gourd rattles. Flutes were also documented in some stories as a courting instrument. The turtle rattles and deer toe rattles were used in ceremonies by the kuseyaay. There were usually more that one kuseyaay in the villages. These men were specialists. One might be an astronomer and know the stars' movements and was aware of the solstices and equinoxes. They let the people know when to harvest various foods. Another might be a healer and herbalist, and yet another might be the hunt kuseyaay and sing and pray to the animals for a good hunt.

Page 30. The Kumeyaay would decorate their bodies in different ways. Tattoos were used in the initiation ceremonies. Charcoal, red and yellow ochres, or white pigments were used to paint lines, circles or dots on the body and face for decorations. Women often decorated their faces and bodies just as women use makeup today.